JIM BRICK

the gift

Project Manager: Jeannette DeLisa
Book Layout: Ken Rehm

Album Art ©1997 Windham Hill Records
Photography: Sandra Johnson
Design: Top Design Studio, Los Angeles

©1997 WARNER BROS. PUBLICATIONS
All Rights Reserved

Contents

THE GIFT

Words and Music by
JIM BRICKMAN and
TOM DOUGLAS

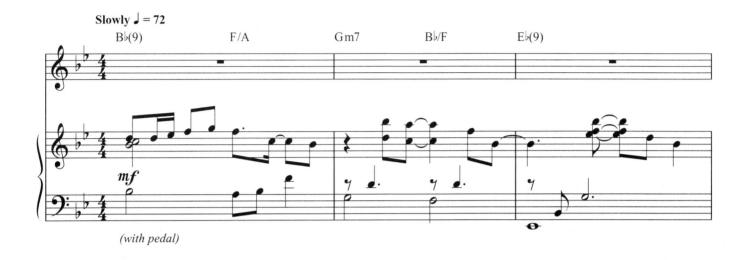

The Gift - 5 - 1
PF9727

4

JOY TO THE WORLD

Traditional
Arranged by JIM BRICKMAN

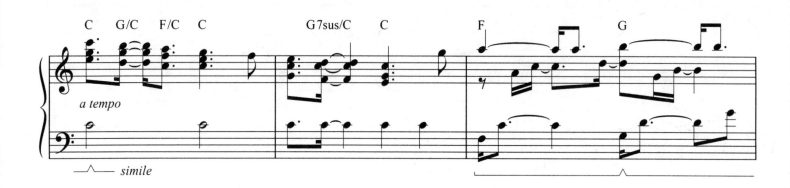

Joy - 4 - 1
PF9727

It Came Upon A Midnight Clear

Traditional
Arranged by JIM BRICKMAN

Flowing, with expression ♩ = 132

It Came Upon A Midnight Clear - 2 - 1
PF9727

It Came Upon A Midnight Clear - 2 - 2
PF9727

Fireside

Composed by
JIM BRICKMAN

Fireside - 4 - 1
PF9727

ANGELS

Composed by
JIM BRICKMAN

Angels - 2 - 1
PF9727

Winter Peace

Composed by
JIM BRICKMAN

Moderately slow, with a free motion ♩ = 78

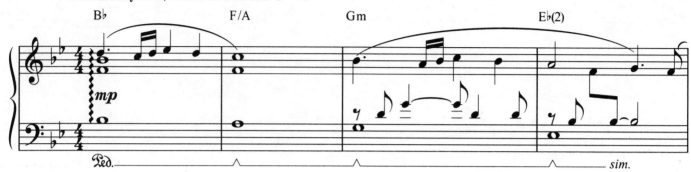

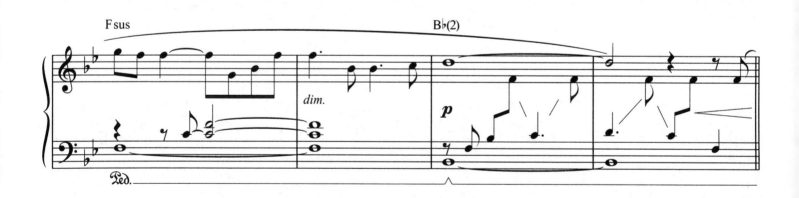

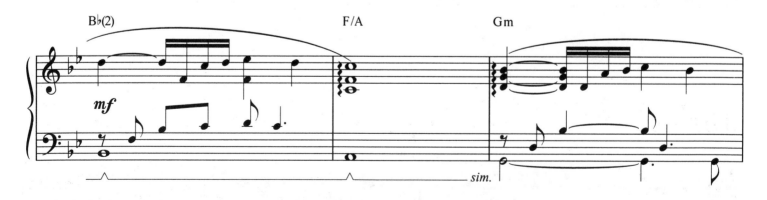

Winter Peace - 4 - 1
PF9727

OH CHRISTMAS TREE

Traditional
Arranged by JIM BRICKMAN

Oh Christmas Tree - 3 - 1
PF9727

the gift

CHORUS:
All I want is to hold you forever
All I need is you more every day
You saved my heart
From being broken apart
You gave your love away
And I'm thankful every day
For the gift

Watching as you softly sleep
What I'd give if I could keep
Just this moment
If only time stood still

But the colors fade away
And the years will make us grey
But baby in my eyes
You'll still be beautiful

CHORUS:
All I want is to hold you forever
All I need is you more every day
You saved my heart
From being broken apart
You gave your love away
And I'm thankful every day
For the gift

(Instrumental)

CHORUS:
All I want is to hold you forever
All I need is you more every day
You saved my heart
From being broken apart
You gave your love away
I can't find the words to say
That I'm thankful everyday
For the gift

Winter snow is falling down
Children laughing all around
lights are turning on
Like a fairy tale come true

Sitting by the fire we made
You're the answer when I prayed
I would find someone
and baby I found you

JIM BRICKMAN

THE FIRST NOEL

Traditional
Arranged by JIM BRICKMAN

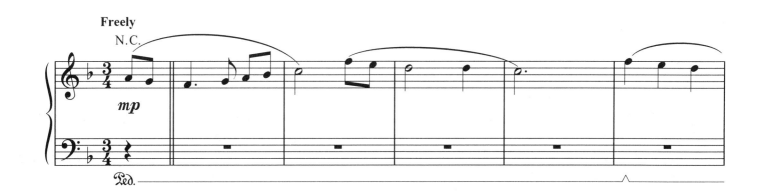

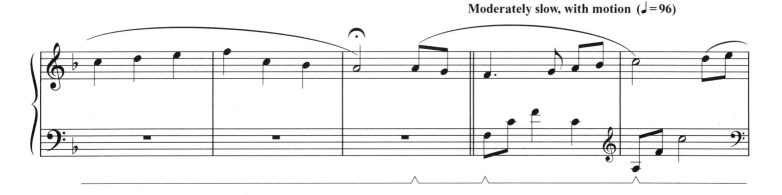

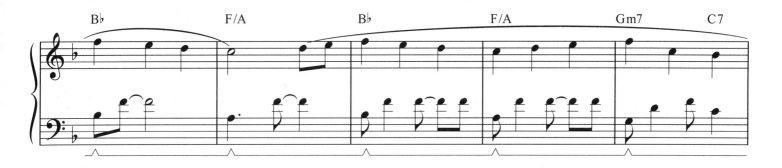

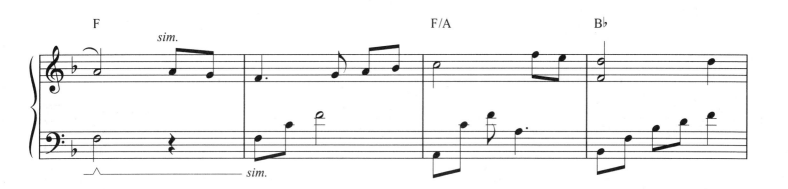

The First Noel - 3 - 1
PF9727

Dreams Come True

Composed by
JIM BRICKMAN

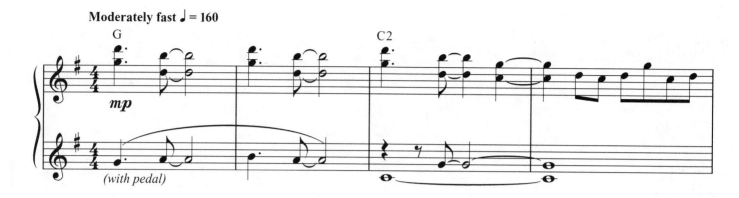

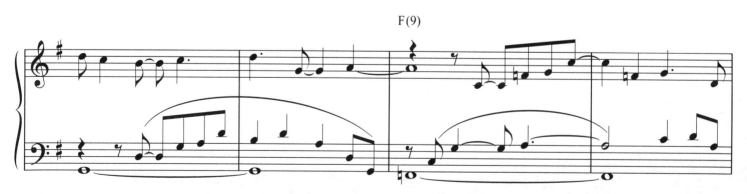

Dreams Come True - 6 - 1
PF9727

Dreams Come True - 6 - 4
PF9727

Dreams Come True - 6 - 6
PF9727

LITTLE TOWN OF BETHLEHEM

Traditional
Arranged by JIM BRICKMAN

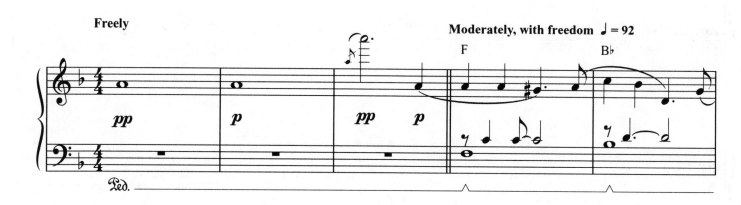

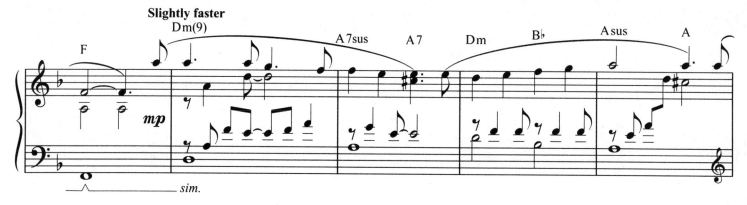

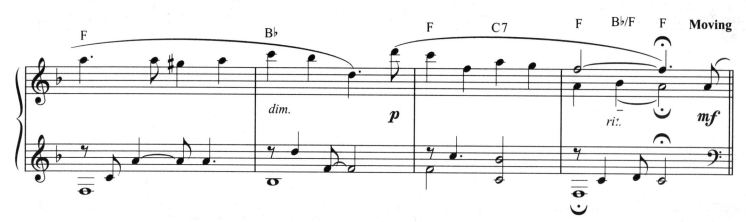

Little Town of Bethlehem - 2 - 1
PF9727

Starbright

Words and Music by
JIM BRICKMAN and
ELLEN WOHL

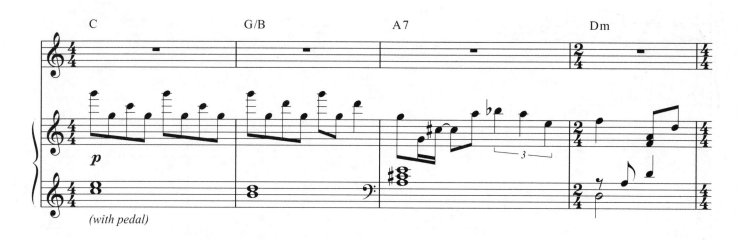

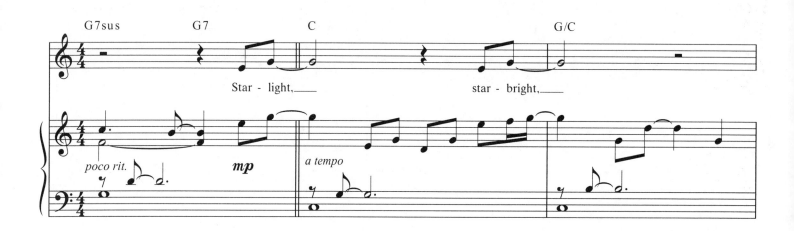

Starbright - 4 - 1
PF9727

44

and you'll a-wak-en on Christ-mas Day.

poco rit.

a tempo

(Star - light,___ star - bright...)

Star - light,___

poco rit.

a tempo

What Child Is This?

Traditional
Arranged by JIM BRICKMAN

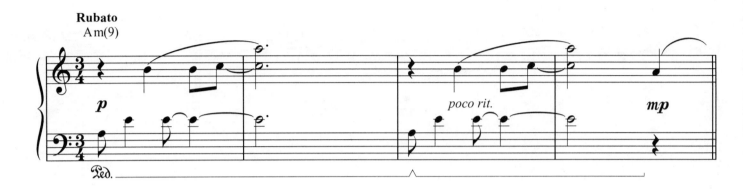

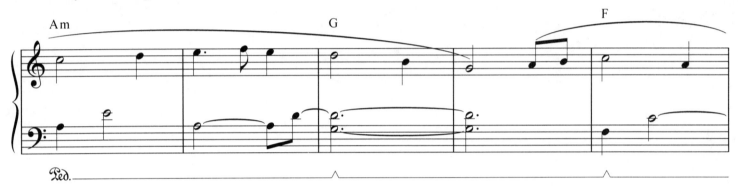

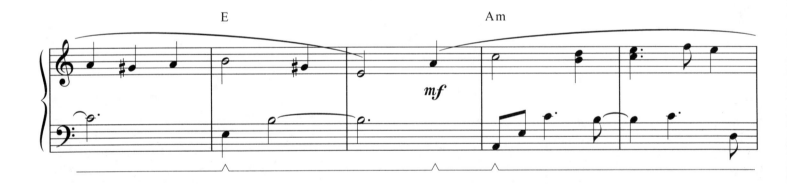

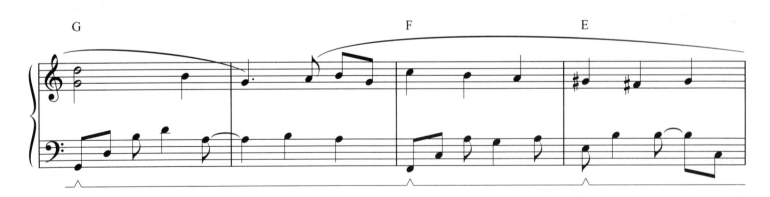

What Child Is This? - 4 - 1
PF9727

What Child Is This? - 4 - 4
PF9727

Hope Is Born Again

Words and Music by
JIM BRICKMAN, BRENT BOURGEOIS,
DOUGLAS KAINE McKELVEY and
BLAIR MASTERS

Moderately slow ♩ = 76

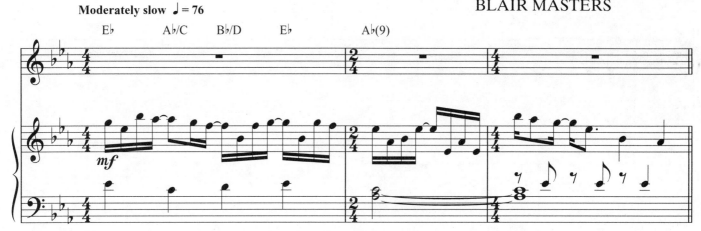

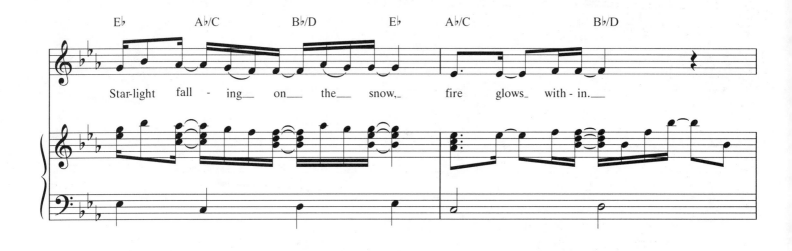

Star-light fall - ing_ on_ the_ snow,_ fire glows_ with - in._

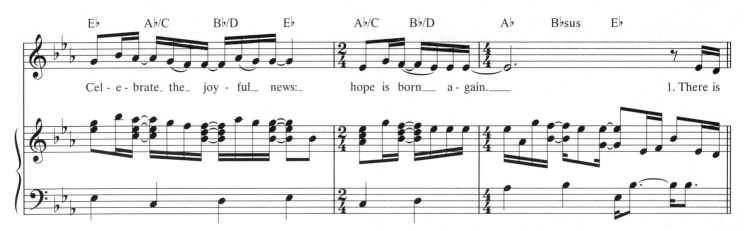

Cel - e - brate_ the_ joy - ful_ news:_ hope is born_ a - gain._

1. There is

Hope Is Born Again - 5 - 1
PF9727

JIM BRICKMAN
the gift

Jim Brickman's original following has grown so substantially that when it came time to record a complete seasonal album, an idea that fans had been wanting for a long time, Jim decided to create something above and beyond the typical seasonal fare. Brickman's gift to us is a balance of carols, original instrumentals and three elegantly produced, orchestrally-enhanced vocal ballads featuring country music star Collin Raye with Susan Ashton on "The Gift," Kenny Loggins ("Starbright"), and gospel group Point of Grace ("Hope Is Born Again"). Those half million plus fans who floated away on the graceful wings of *Picture This* will also enjoy a powerful, soulful reworking of that album's lead track, "Dream Come True."

Brickman enjoyed great success in early 1997 with the crossover country/pop vocal ballad "Valentine," with vocalist Martina McBride. His affinity for the artistry of country music made working with Collin Raye and Susan Ashton an especially rewarding experience. "What I was trying to do on both 'Valentine' and 'The Gift' was bring artists of different genres together, and cross these amazing singers over into my world of solo piano-based material," he says. "Country has some of the best ballad singers and some of the greatest emotional honesty in all of music, and I felt that fit in well with my sound. It's truly gratifying to bring these together."

Brickman put a lot of thought into the instrumentals as well. A native of Cleveland and those snowy Midwest winters, Brickman found the perfect white Christmas memories to use as inspiration for these. "It was important for me to infuse my own viewpoint of winter and the holidays into this collection, to paint vivid pictures of my own," he says. "To convey what winter sounded and looked like to me. As I see them, they are not simply Christmas songs, but about human relationships, special people and family. The religious aspects of the holidays make us more aware of them."

"In fact," Brickman adds, "the whole idea of the song 'The Gift' and naming the album after it comes from my belief that it's not so much about the actual tangible stuff people give each other as the experience of sharing, the love that goes with that. The music here is telling the story of people interacting in as tasteful a manner as possible."

"Covering the traditional ballads was an unusual process for me, since I have never done outside material before," says Brickman of his bright, jazzy renditions of "It Came Upon A Midnight Clear," "What Child Is This," "The First Noel," "Oh Christmas Tree" and "O Little Town of Bethlehem." "The challenge was not to force any new twists, to simply let things flow and play them like I would an original piece. I began by finding a comfortable key and then finding spots where I felt improvisation might work. I associate many of these songs with vocal versions, and doing them instrumentally opens up numerous possibilities. It was also important to choose songs with a hymn-like quality, ancient rather than modern classics. The simpler, the better."

It is this commitment to honest, emotional musicianship that is the key to Brickman's astounding success story. Brickman's simple yet heart-tugging musical statements have been breaking down genre walls since his second Windham Hill album, 1995's *By Heart*. That album spawned three top ten singles ("Angel Eyes," "If You Believe," "By Heart") which hit the vocal-oriented adult contemporary charts. He has with all three albums (beginning with his breakthrough *No Words* in 1994) had extraordinary success throughout the country as the only solo pop piano player on soft rock stations.

Brickman's ability to convey the point of a song within a few bars can be traced to his successful longtime jingle writing business, Brickman Arrangement, which the pianist founded while juggling business classes at Case Western Reserve University with classical composition and performance courses at the Cleveland Institute of Music. Over the years, his familiar accounts grew to include Standard Oil, McDonald's, Pontiac, 7-Up, AT&T, Purina Puppy Chow, The Gap and the Walt Disney Company.

"I think people respond to my music because I really play what I feel," says Brickman. "What you hear in each song is my heart and soul pouring out without any pretensions of trying to impress the listener with any clever tricks. I like to feel as though I am sitting in someone's house, playing the piano for them one on one."

Jim Brickman's *The Gift* will make us feel all of the picture-perfect emotions of the season, as seen through the eyes of an artist who has become one of our generation's greatest piano playing romantics.

JIM BRICKMAN

INCLUDE:

SOLO ALBUMS:
NO WORDS

BY HEART

PICTURE THIS

THE GIFT

COMPILATIONS:
PIANO SAMPLER 2

A WINTER SOLSTICE V & VI

WINDHAM HILL SAMPLER 1996 & 1997

THE CAROLS OF CHRISTMAS

JIM BRICKMAN would like to invite you to be on his Mailing List to receive information about concert schedules, merchandise and upcoming releases. Please fill out the coupon below and mail to:

JIM BRICKMAN
c/o EDGE ENTERTAINMENT
11288 VENTURA BLVD. SUITE 606
STUDIO CITY, CA 91604

(818) 508-8400 phone
(213) 876-6815 fax
        or
E-Mail us at BrickPiano@AOL.com. or call 1-888-BRICKMAN for **VIP Club Membership**, concert tour and merchandise information.
Find Jim Brickman's Web Page at www.Windham.com.

Cut Along Here ✂

NAME _____

ADDRESS _____

CITY_____ **STATE** _____ **ZIP**_____

DOB:_____ **E-Mail**_____

                         Phone:_____

I first heard about Jim Brickman's music _____

_____

THE GIFT